Lily The Grasshopper

Nancy P Best

Written by Nancy Pulling Best

Illustrated by Mathew S. Capron

Lily The Grasshopper

by Nancy Pulling Best

June 2018

Illustrations and Illustration Editing by Mathew S. Capron
Raleigh, North Carolina

Published by
Petrie Press
A Division of Nancy Did It
2985 Powell Road
Blossvale NY 13308
www.nancydidit.com

Printed in the United States of America
by Versa Press

ISBN 978-0-9711638-8-1

Dedications

This book is dedicated to my friend Jay O'Hern. He is an amazing man who never stops writing. He is not young but that never stops him. He has been coming to the Adirondacks since he was a very young child and he never tires of telling stories of the people and places there. I only hope I can continue to write for my whole life just like he has.

Nancy Pulling Best

Jay O'Hern

To my fantastic daughter, as always, for being my inspiration to keep on keeping on. I'd also like to send a special Thank You to all of my friends on the interwebz for all the support they give me with my art. It's a grcat feeling to know my works bring joy to so many others. That's what it is really all about!

Mathew S. Capron

Lily was a grasshopper.
She was lots of fun.

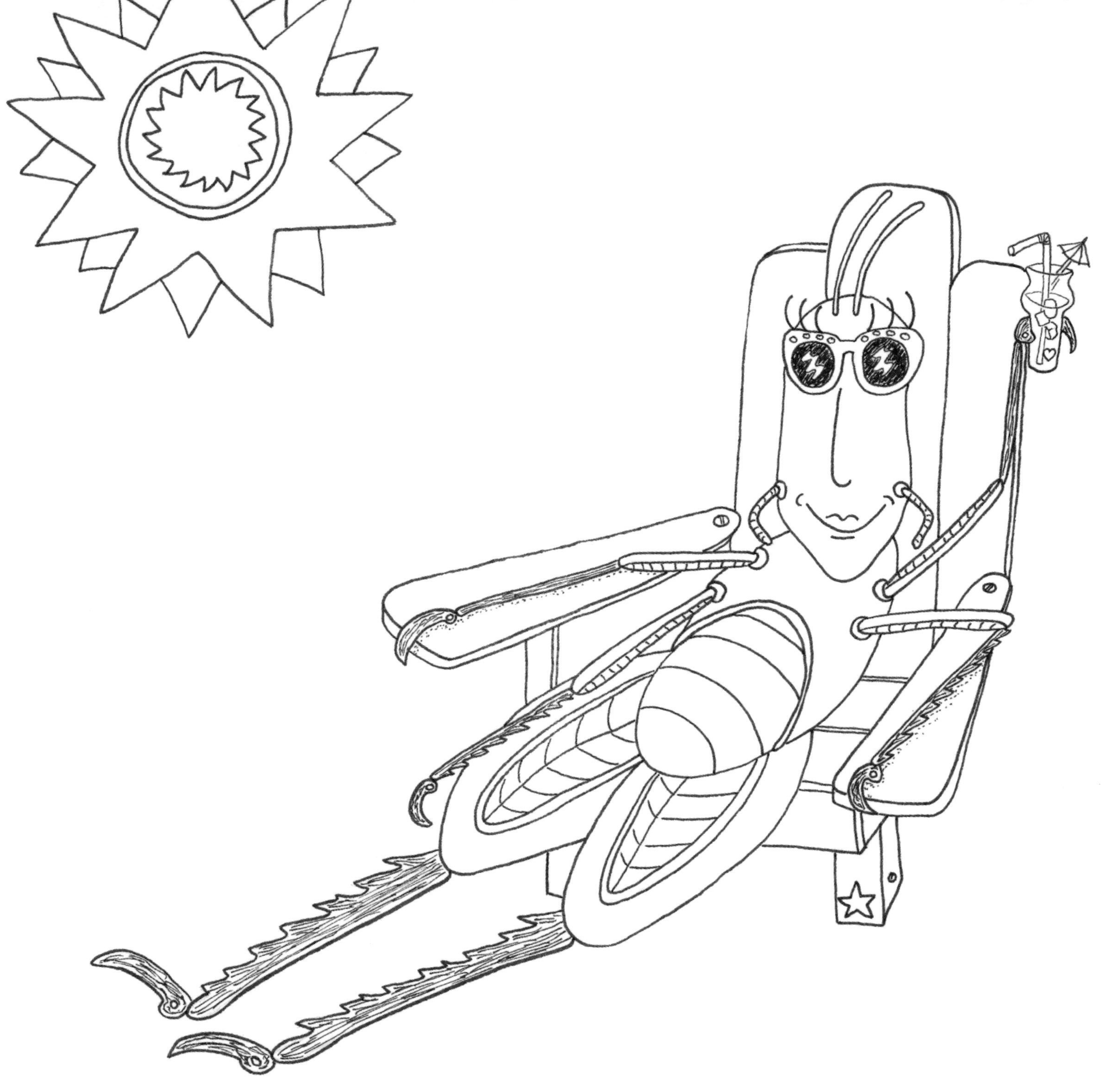

Lily liked to lay
out in the
Adirondack sun.

Jumping was her specialty but she could also fly.

With six legs and her four wings she could reach the sky.

One day while she was sunning on a big flat rock,

A giant bullfrog came along and he began to mock.

He said he could jump really far and that he was the best.

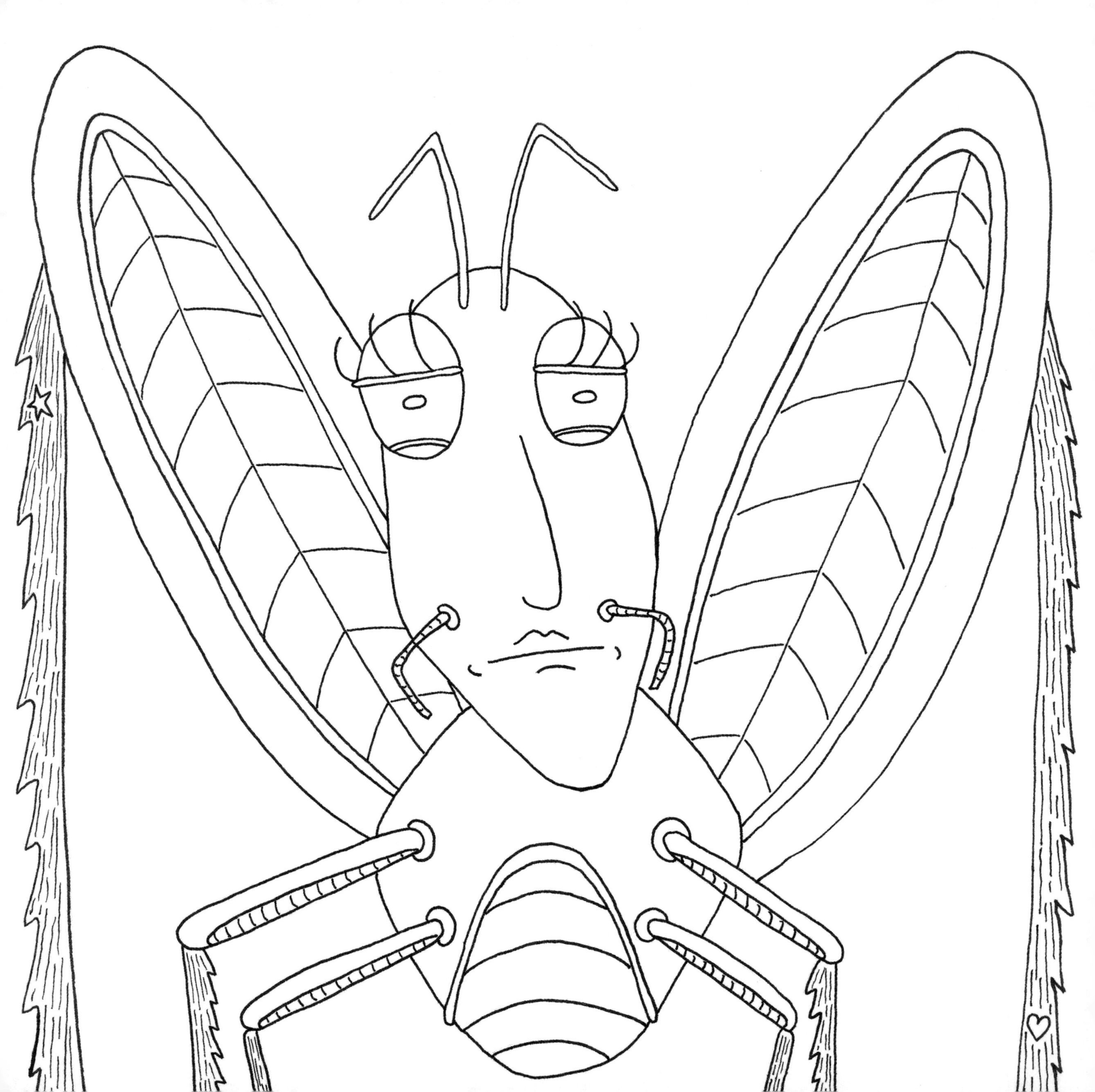

Lily took offense at that and put him to the test.

They picked a date for jumping and invited all their friends. The salamanders were in charge of all the odds and ends.

They set up chairs, brought in drinks and even took some bets. The event was well attended. It was as good as it could get.

Lily let the frog go first. It was only fair.

Then Lily took a turn and beat him by a hair.

START

He said, “How ‘bout best of three?” and Lily said, “Alright.” Then he went right back to the start and jumped with all his might

He did well but didn't know what the grasshopper could do.

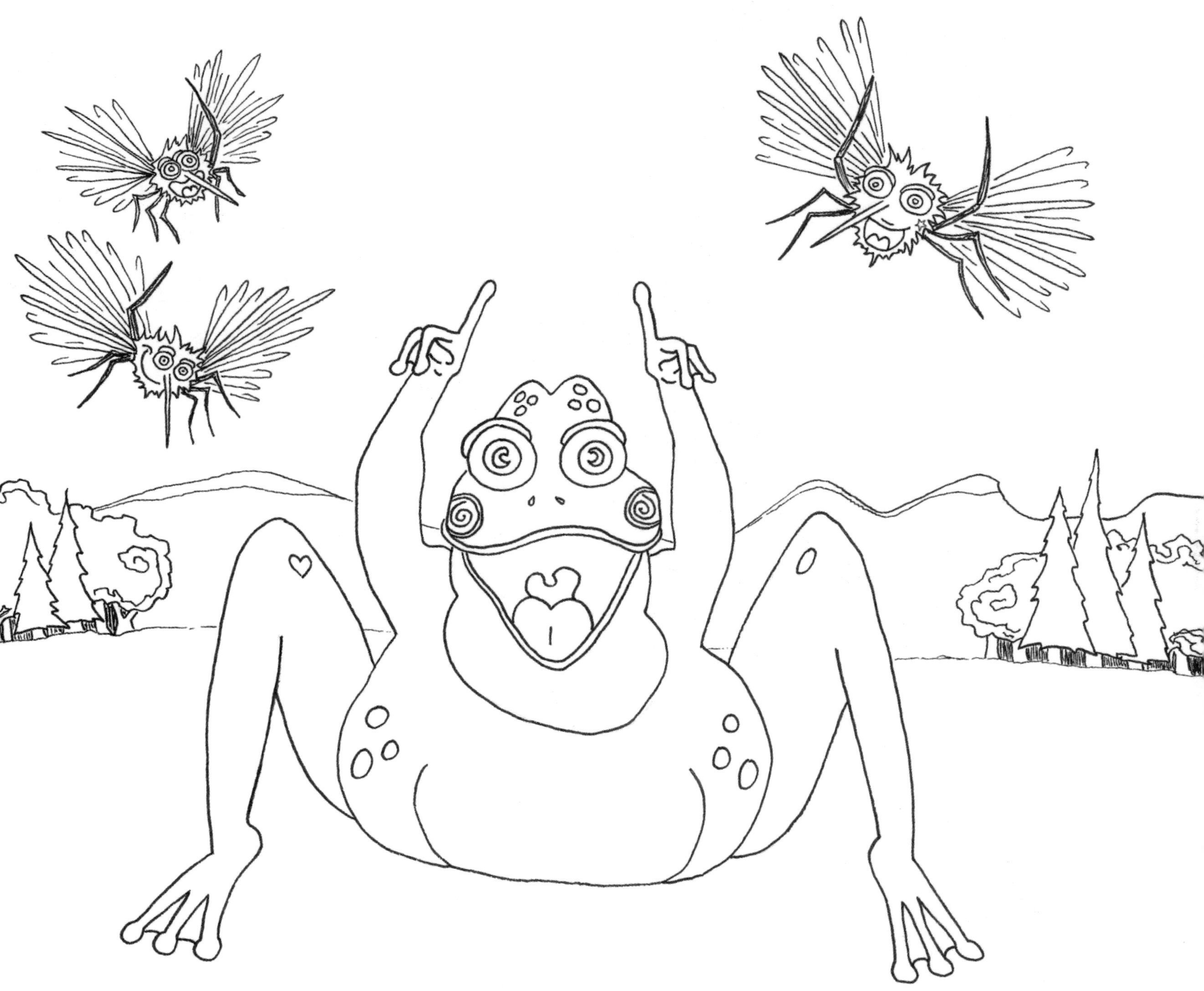

She stepped up to the line, Lily jumped and then she flew.

It was the best jump she had ever done. Everyone clapped for they knew the grasshopper had won.

Meet The Author: Nancy Pulling Best

Born and raised in the Adirondack mountains in upstate New York, Nancy prides herself in being a 4th generation Adirondacker.

"My great grandparents, grandparents, parents, children and 1st grandchild were all from the Old Forge, area in the Adirondacks," Best said.

After writing for her own personal use, newspapers and magazines, she brings you her fourth children's book.

She also authored "Anna the Spider," "Pepper the Dragonfly," "Bob the Bumblebee," "Learning To Cook Adirondack" and "Learning To Cook Adirondack Over An Open Fire." They are all available at www.nancydidit.com

Meet The Illustrator: Mathew S. Capron

Born and raised in the Adirondack mountains in upstate New York and now residing in the Carolinas, Mat always had a love for art and found a lot of peace in it.

He is the father of a beautiful daughter, who also enjoys being creative.

"I'm happy to have had an opportunity to illustrate this book," Mat said. "I hope you find happiness and peace within."

Mat also illustrated "Anna The Spider" "Pepper The Dragonfly" and "Bob the Bumble-bee." More art and illustrations by M@ can be found at... hew-Art.com

Lily hopes to see you around and do some jumping...

@mapron